22nd Century

FUTURE OF SPACE

Stephanie Paris

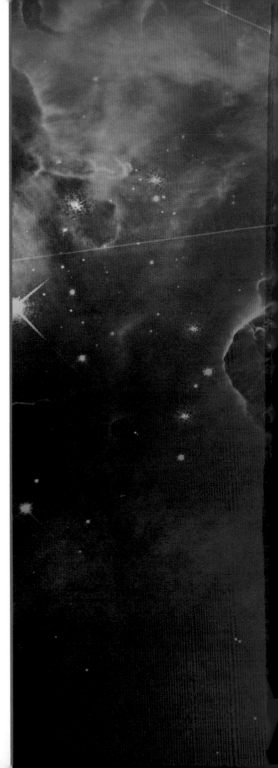

Consultants

Timothy Rasinski, Ph.D.
Kent State University

Lori Oczkus
Literacy Consultant

Based on writing from
TIME For Kids. TIME For Kids and the *TIME
For Kids* logo are registered trademarks of
TIME Inc. Used under license.

Publishing Credits

Dona Herweck Rice, *Editor-in-Chief*
Lee Aucoin, *Creative Director*
Jamey Acosta, *Senior Editor*
Lexa Hoang, *Designer*
Stephanie Reid, *Photo Editor*
Rane Anderson, *Contributing Author*
Rachelle Cracchiolo, *M.S.Ed., Publisher*

Image Credits: pp.18, 38, 49 (bottom)
iStockphoto; pp.2–3, 6, 6–7, 16, 16–17,
46–47, 56–57 NASA; pp.10, 10–11, 17, 25,
34 (bottom) PhotoResearchers Inc.; p.15
REUTERS/Newscom p.22 TVO/Newscom
pp.34–35 (steps1-4) Daein Ballard
(CC BY-SA); pp.12–13, 23, 28–31, 40–43,
46–47 (illustrations) Timothy J. Bradley;
All other images from Shutterstock.

Teacher Created Materials

5301 Oceanus Drive
Huntington Beach, CA 92649-1030
http://www.tcmpub.com
ISBN 978-1-4333-4901-0
© 2013 Teacher Created Materials, Inc.

TABLE OF CONTENTS

THE FUTURE OF SPACE

In the movies, humans often explore deep space. They travel faster than the speed of light. Landing on strange planets and meeting **aliens** is all in a day's work.

In real life, technology is limited. But scientists are searching for **habitable** planets. They are looking for signs of **intelligent life**. And they are working on making space travel much faster so we can travel greater distances. But three things need to happen before we can travel into deep space as they do in the movies. First, we need to travel much faster. But we can't go far without fuel. And fuel is heavy. Somehow, we must power long-distance voyages without running out of fuel. And finally, we need to power the space vehicle once it's in space. Today, scientists are focused on making **breakthroughs** on these three problems.

THINK LINK

- What breakthroughs in technology will help us travel deeper into space?

- What new technologies will help us build better space vehicles?

- What might we find as we travel into space in the 22nd century?

It's hard to say what will happen. Not even the National Aeronautics and Space Administration (NASA) plans more than 30 years ahead! But all the ideas in this book are based on real science. Life today is very different than it was a hundred years ago. And it's hard to know what will happen in the next hundred years. One thing is certain. Much of what is science fiction today will be reality tomorrow.

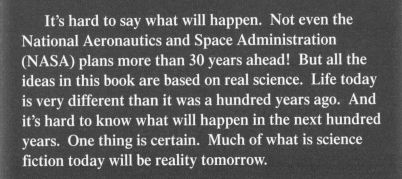

HOW FAR WE'VE GONE

The space probe Voyager 1 has traveled farther than any other spacecraft from Earth. It took over 20 years for it to reach the edge of our solar system.

Voyager 1

How Far is Far?

A light-year is equal to the distance light travels in one year, about 5.8 trillion miles.

Proxima Centauri
4.2 light-years away from Earth

moon
0.0000000406 light-years from the sun

sun
0.000016 light-years from Earth

NEW TECHNOLOGY

New inventions can be simple or complex. But the best ones make our lives easier. They allow us to do things we couldn't do before. Today, we no longer rely solely on telescopes to learn about space. Now, we can send rockets into space. We can land robots on distant planets. Humans can live on space stations. And this is just the beginning.

New technology comes from new ideas. Nearly every invention requires creativity. Mistakes will be made. But there will also be successes. Scientists are merging current technology with imagination. They plan to invent technology that is out of this world!

FUTURISTS

Futurists are people who take what we know today and try to imagine where it might lead in the future. Not everything they come up with happens, of course. But their ideas often guide research going forward.

PAST PREDICTIONS

In the past, futurists predicted that by today we would have:

flying cars   electronic money   time machines

intelligence pills   computers in every home

cities in the sky

shopping by computer   artificial human organs

Which of their predictions have come true so far?

ROBONAUTS

Engineers build robots to explore places that are currently too dangerous for astronauts. They can go farther and faster than humans. Some robots take photographs of planets as they fly by. Some have wheels so they can roll over the surface of a planet to collect **data**. Robots have explored Mars, Venus, Jupiter, and the moon.

NASA is building robots to look like people. They call them *robonauts*. These robots have hands that move like human hands. Some futurists predict that human-looking robots will be programmed to think, move, and act like humans. Scientists believe human-like robots will be used on Earth as well as in space.

THE TURING TEST

In the 1950s, computer scientist Alan Turing proposed a way to judge **artificial intelligence (AI)**. He suggested having a person ask questions of a computer and another human. If the questioner is unable to tell which is which, then the computer has passed the test and is said to be intelligent! (Since a computer's voice would give it away, usually both the human and the computer communicate with written text on a screen.)

AI

People are fascinated by the idea of artificial intelligence. This refers to the ways that machines "think." They aren't alive, but they can learn new information and make decisions.

Mars rover Curiosity

Of the 450 astronauts who have traveled into space, 45 of them have died during their missions. In the future, robots will be able to help save lives.

THE THREE LAWS OF ROBOTICS

Futurist and author Isaac Asimov developed three laws of robotics in 1942. They are designed to make working with robots as successful as possible.

I

A robot may not injure a human or, through inaction, allow a human to come to harm.

ROBOTS ON MARS

The rover Curiosity landed on Mars in 2012. The robot is equipped with cameras that will send back images of areas on Mars that have never been explored. The rover also includes many tools designed to help scientists search for signs of alien life.

2

A robot must obey the orders given to it by humans except where such orders would conflict with the First Law.

3

A robot must protect its own existence as long as such protection does not conflict with the First or Second Laws.

TINY TECH

Have you seen a replicator in a science-fiction movie? These machines can make almost anything from nothing. Seems impossible, right? Futurists aren't so sure.

Today, we are learning about **nanotechnology**. The ability to build things from molecules and atoms is an exciting possibility. Scientists are trying to build a **morphing** spacecraft with nanotechnology. This kind of ship could change shape as it flies. These aircrafts would burn less fuel, fly longer, and change direction easily. They could morph into whatever shape works best in different areas of space.

What if we could go even smaller? What if we could work with parts of atoms? **Femtotechnology** will allow us to build whatever atoms we need from scratch. With that, we really could make almost anything from nothing!

an industrial robot

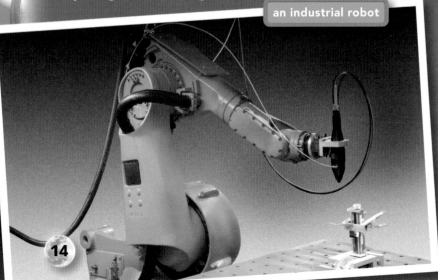

3-D printers are machines that can scan a tool or other object and reproduce it. This isn't science fiction. It's real! Imagine needing another little robot to help you on your spaceship. Your onboard 3-D printer could make one for you.

a nano-size race car model created by a 3-D printer

SOLAR POWER

Have you seen solar panels on roofs around town? They are used to make energy from the sun. That energy powers our homes and schools. It is a form of **renewable** energy. With solar power, spacecrafts could avoid carrying heavy amounts of fuel. And they could travel farther without having to refuel. Instead of using fuel, a **light sail craft** could use small particles of light for energy. These **photons** would drive the ship. The speed of the photons could push the ship forward and provide energy.

SOLAR SAILS

As the name suggests, solar sail crafts would have large sails. The sails might be over 100 feet wide! They would be made of a super-thin film of plastic or aluminum.

a solar-powered aircraft

Using solar sails, Japan has successfully sent a spacecraft at top speeds to the planet Venus and beyond.

TELEPORTERS

The fastest way to get from place to place may be **teleportation**. Scientists are working on moving matter quickly from one place to another. A machine may be able to reduce your body to tiny particles. In less than a second, it could send you off to school where you would resume your normal shape. Futurists believe by the middle of the next century, we will be able to build teleporters. Rockets will be **obsolete**. To travel through the **galaxy**, astronauts would simply pick a planet and pack their bags!

"BEAM ME UP, SCOTTY!"

Star Trek, a popular TV show in the 1960s, used the idea of teleporting to move members of the crew on and off spaceships. After stepping onto a transporter, the person's body was separated into atoms until it reached its destination. At that point, the atoms were put back together. Fiction may one day be reality!

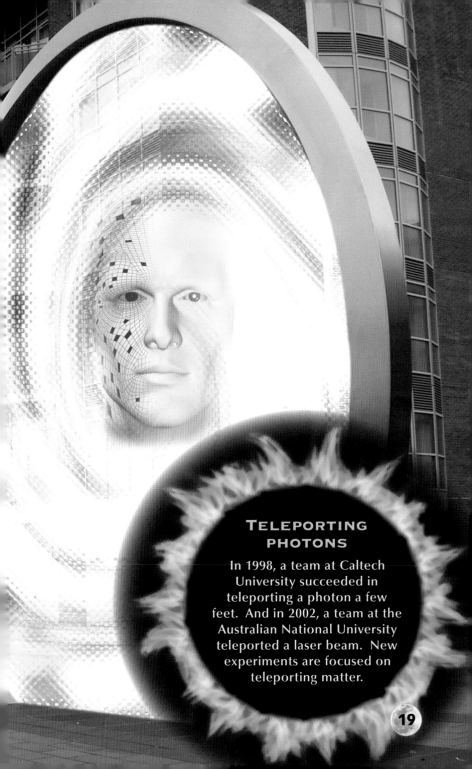

TELEPORTING PHOTONS

In 1998, a team at Caltech University succeeded in teleporting a photon a few feet. And in 2002, a team at the Australian National University teleported a laser beam. New experiments are focused on teleporting matter.

ENERGY

$E=MC^2$ may be the most famous formula in the world. One thing it says is that energy and mass are the same thing. They can change back and forth. The transformation is very powerful. One kilogram of water could power a car for 100,000 years without stopping. If we could change matter into energy, we would have an unlimited supply!

ANTIMATTER

New advances in **antimatter** technology may allow spaceships to make their own fuel. Antimatter is the opposite of matter. It is matter with a negative charge. Scientists have been able to make small amounts in laboratories. When exposed to matter, antimatter changes all the mass into energy. This could make any kind of matter into efficient fuel. But since antimatter instantly destroys itself and other matter, it doesn't last very long. That's just one of the kinks that still need to be worked out.

Energy

Energy is the capacity to do work or cause changes. It comes in many forms and changes from one form to another.

Mass

This is the amount of matter in an object.

Speed of Light

C stands for the maximum possible speed in the **universe**, or about 186,000 miles per second.

$$E=mc^2$$

Squared

Squaring is multiplying a number by itself. The enormous size of c^2 means that a tiny object can produce a vast amount of energy.

Equals

Albert Einstein realized energy and mass are related.

NEW WORLDS

Many scientists are concerned about Earth's future. They worry about climate change and **overpopulation**. Futurists know we will need to travel beyond Earth to meet our needs. In a billion years, the sun will be getting hotter. Our oceans will start to dry up. The planet will become uninhabitable. It will be time to move on! This day may come sooner if the Earth's resources are used too quickly. But if humans can't live on Earth, where can they live?

"Our only chance of long-term survival is not to remain inward looking on planet Earth but to spread out into space."
— astrophysicist Stephen Hawking, speaking in 2010

THERE'S NO PLACE LIKE HOME

Humans are like Goldilocks. Our home can't be too hot or too cold. Gravity can't be too strong or too weak. The air can't have too much or too little oxygen. In many ways, Earth is just right for humans.

Earth is just the right distance from the sun. It isn't deathly hot like Mercury or frozen like Neptune.

About 70 percent of Earth's surface is covered with water—an ingredient many scientists believe is essential for life.

The planet's **atmosphere** protects us from the sun's harmful rays and keeps Earth at a steady temperature. Air also allows sound waves to travel, which lets us talk with one another.

SPACE ELEVATOR

The best place to look for new planets is from space. One way for people to travel into space may be on a space elevator. The elevator would use nanotechnology and advanced AI. It would extend thousands of miles into space. Ordinary people could travel easily beyond Earth's atmosphere. From there, they could catch a ride to a space station, the moon, or even Mars. The space elevator may be the first stop as humans explore the galaxy.

DOLLARS AND SENSE

A space elevator would be much less expensive than a rocket. On a rocket, it costs thousands of dollars to send a single pound of material into space. Every trip on an elevator would cost thousands of dollars less. If travel is less expensive, it would be possible to send more materials into space. With more resources in space, more ships and stations could be built.

"The space elevator will be built about 50 years after everyone stops laughing."
—Arthur C. Clarke, futurist

NEXT STOP: THE STARS!

Sit back and relax. You're on board a space elevator attached to a cable that is taking you thousands of miles into space. As the elevator begins to rise, you look out the window to see the ground moving away below you. The cities begin to shrink. You become aware of the weather patterns over the land and ocean. And you begin to notice the curvature of Earth. The blue of the sky darkens as your elevator ride takes you out into space. Next stop: the stars!

LARGE SPACE STATIONS

Today, the International Space Station (ISS) is the largest artificial satellite in the sky. But only a few scientists can live and work there at one time. In the future, space stations may be huge cities in the sky. They could house researchers and their families. Space stations of the future may have advanced power plants at their core. They will probably have **artificial gravity**. It would prevent people from floating.

A GRAVE MATTER

Living without gravity is hard on human bodies. Our muscles and bones are designed to work on Earth. In space, astronauts must exercise for several hours a day to keep their muscles toned.

The interior of a futuristic space station may include large windows for stargazing.

DIG DEEPER!

SPACE ARCHITECT

Imagine you and your family are going to live on a huge space station orbiting Earth. You'll need gravity, oxygen, food, and water. But what else does the place need to feel like home? Think about the sort of station you would like to live on. Draw a floor plan or blueprint for your space station. Use pieces of paper, straws, yarn, foam, modeling clay, or other items to make your design come to life.

solar panels

docking port

living quarters

equipment and storage supplies

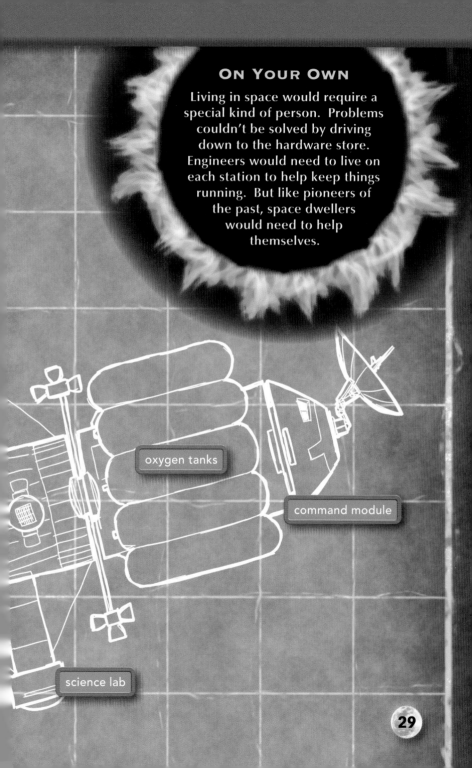

ON YOUR OWN

Living in space would require a special kind of person. Problems couldn't be solved by driving down to the hardware store. Engineers would need to live on each station to help keep things running. But like pioneers of the past, space dwellers would need to help themselves.

oxygen tanks

command module

science lab

COLONY ON THE MOON

Space stations wouldn't be the only places to live. Most futurists think there will be colonies on the moon. These would make more room for the growing number of people on Earth. Pioneers could live in small domed cities. Most of what we would need could be grown on the moon itself. The rest would be brought up from Earth to get us started.

Right now, scientists are looking at creating small lunar outposts on the moon. These would help scientists study what it might be like to visit other planets. And they would tell us what may be needed for future colonies.

People could use an electric monorail to travel through the colony.

Children of the crew members and researchers would attend school. Class topics may include solar geography, lunar history, and USL (Universal Space Language).

Indoor farms would be used for growing food.

INSIDE A MOON COLONY

What would life be like inside a lunar city? This is just one way futurists think a moon colony may look.

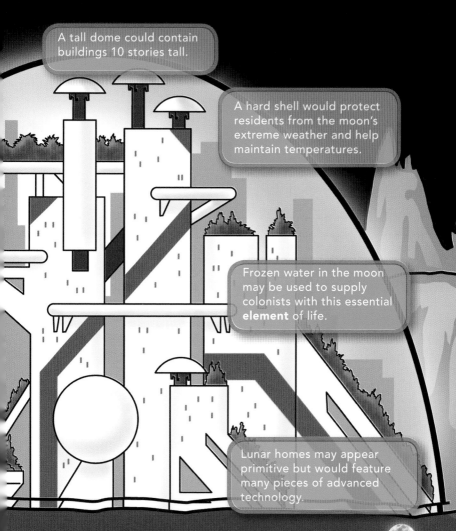

A tall dome could contain buildings 10 stories tall.

A hard shell would protect residents from the moon's extreme weather and help maintain temperatures.

Frozen water in the moon may be used to supply colonists with this essential **element** of life.

Lunar homes may appear primitive but would feature many pieces of advanced technology.

Mars is very different from Earth. But futurists are eyeing Mars. With some work, some think it could be transformed into a place where life thrives. **Terraforming** is the practice of transforming a hostile planet into somewhere humans can live. Future technology may allow us to make over Mars into a habitable place.

Mars is a unique planet with its own history—and perhaps even its own life. Some people believe it would be wrong to change Mars in ways that could make it less Mars-like. Others believe that may be the only way for humans to survive.

Scientists have built closed environments on Earth to test how we might live on another planet.

A NEW HOME

Imagine living in a small room with three other people for years at a time. The first colonists on Mars will need to be mentally and emotionally ready to survive some tough times. Maintaining air, water, and food supplies as well as creating a comfortable home will all take time and impressive problem-solving skills. And when problems arise, everyone will know there's no going back!

Terraforming Mars would require building places to grow food and other plants.

MAKING MARS OUR OWN

Terraforming Mars would require four big steps. Explorers will focus on creating three main elements: water, energy, and life.

Step 1

Build up Mars's currently thin atmosphere with man-made gases. This would protect life from dangerous UV rays. It would also raise the temperature of the planet.

Step 2

Melt the polar ice caps to make liquid water. This would make carbon dioxide gas, too. And it would make the temperature of the planet warmer.

Step 3

Bring life to the planet to create an ecosystem.

Step 4

Eventually, the air would become breathable for humans.

How long would terraforming Mars take? Estimates vary widely from 50 years to over 100 million years!

NEW NEIGHBORS

Our solar system is just one tiny area of the Milky Way galaxy. And the Milky Way is just one of billions of galaxies in the universe. **Exoplanets** orbit stars beyond our sun. If we find Earth-like exoplanets, we may be able to colonize or mine them. If we found life on another planet, it would be one of the biggest discoveries ever made. But what would it mean for life on Earth?

WHERE TO LOOK

Scientists search for life on rocky planets that are warm but not too hot and have liquid water—just like Earth.

"Two possibilities exist: either we are alone in the universe or we are not. Both are equally terrifying."
—Arthur C. Clarke

LIFE

Much of the science in the 22nd century will be driven by the search for alien life. Scientists think it will have at least two things in common with us. It will need water. Until recently, scientists thought this water had to be liquid. But the discovery of live bacteria that had been frozen for 30,000 years has challenged this idea. Experts also expect life will include the element carbon. This is because carbon atoms form long chains that are useful for building living things.

Carbon atoms can join together to become the building blocks for life.

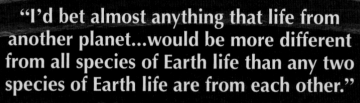

> "I'd bet almost anything that life from another planet...would be more different from all species of Earth life than any two species of Earth life are from each other."
>
> —Neil deGrasse Tyson, astrophysicist

FRIEND OR FOE?

If intelligent life came to Earth, would it be friendly? Some scientists believe that if an alien civilization comes to Earth, then it will be here for our resources. Others think there is much we could learn from such advanced creatures.

DIG DEEPER!

DEFINING LIFE

What is life? Many great minds have tried to come up with a working definition, but there are problems with each. No one seems able to agree. Still, if an alien race flew up to us on a spaceship and waved hello, most people would call it intelligent life. Scientist Carl Sagan listed five qualities needed for life. Each one has a flaw. But when you put them all together, they make up life as we know it.

01011
10100
10100

Genes

Life uses **genes** to pass on information.

 but

A computer virus can be designed to pass on information. Is it alive?

Physical

Life is anything that can act. Eating, moving, breathing, growing, and responding are but all actions.

Does that mean that a moving car is alive?

Energy

Life uses energy to exist.

but → Is a lightbulb that uses energy alive?

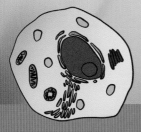

Order

Life is contained in a location. It increases order.

but → Libraries increase the order of books. Does that make them alive?

Chemical

DNA is used to produce the next generation of life.

but → A mule is the child of a donkey and a horse. It cannot reproduce. Does that mean it isn't alive?

ALIEN LIFE FORMS

When you think of the word *alien,* what comes to mind? Is it a hairless creature with pale skin and big, black, slanted eyes? In movies and books, aliens often appear very much like humans. They have arms and legs. They walk upright like humans. But there's really no telling what types of aliens exist in the universe until we actually meet them. They may be as tiny as a freckle or as large as an ocean. They could be tall and skinny without eyes. They could fly like birds and have tentacles for eyes.

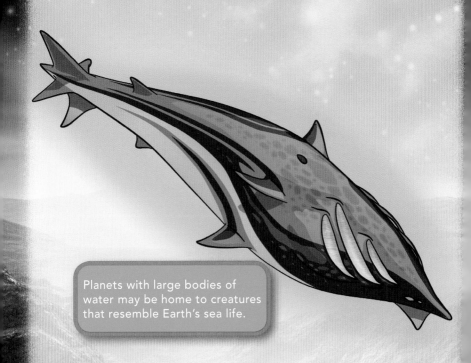

Planets with large bodies of water may be home to creatures that resemble Earth's sea life.

Large gasbag aliens may thrive on gases that are poisonous to humans.

Planets with little light may develop creatures with large eyes to absorb light from a distant star.

Planets with short plants may host grazing animals similar to elephants or cows.

NEW UNIVERSES

What is the universe? What is space? These are basic questions. Yet they remain among the most mysterious. The universe is made up of stars, planets, matter, light, energy, and time. It contains everything. But what shape is it? How big is it? What is the stuff that is between all the stuff? How did it begin, and how will it end? Scientists have theories that explain some of this. But no one knows for sure.

MULTIVERSE

Some scientists think that our universe may only be one of many. These universes may all bump up against each other with edges that connect like bubbles. It might even be possible to travel between them. But the rules of other universes may not be like our own. Gravity might push away. And up might actually be down!

"Let your soul stand cool and composed before a million universes."
—Walt Whitman, poet

PARALLEL WORLDS

There are many theories that have led scientists to wonder if **parallel universes** may exist. One theory holds that whenever we have a choice to make, every choice that can be made is made. If it's true, every time we make a decision, the world changes, and a new universe splits off from our own. A new reality is created, and both choices are made. The differences can be really small, like when you wear a red shirt instead of a green shirt. Or the differences can be epic—what if the asteroid that killed the dinosaurs missed Earth? Would humans have ever evolved?

To Saturn or Mars?

Left or right?

STOP! THINK...

- Do you think parallel universes exist?

- How might scientists test this theory?

- If there are multiple versions of you, living multiple lives, would one of you be the true you?

Love or hate?

Hello or goodbye?

Height, width, and depth are familiar dimensions. They tell where something is. Time can be thought of as another dimension. It tells *when* something is. But scientists think there may be more dimensions. They may be so tiny that they only exist on the subatomic level. If we could travel to a new dimension, we might find a whole new world.

KEEPING COUNT

Scientists believe there may be either six or seven other dimensions. That would mean there may be as many as 11 total! One theory says that they are all curled up on top of each other. This would make them very difficult for us to find.

TRY THIS

It's difficult to picture multiple dimensions. Even the experts have no idea what 11 dimensions would look like. But one way to start is by thinking about a triangle. Now imagine tipping it backwards. From this angle, it looks like a flat line. But what if you turn it to the side? You may find it's a pyramid. If you only look at it from one perspective, you can't see its true shape.

line
one dimension

triangle
two dimensions

pyramid
three dimensions

BLACK HOLES

Black holes are some of the most mysterious objects in space. Scientists don't understand them. But they know they exist. They are formed when large stars end their lives. The smallest black holes are just a few times the size of our sun. Astronomers think a black hole may lie at the center of every galaxy.

Scientists want to know more about these strange places. But traveling close to a black hole poses a problem. Gravity is so strong in these areas that it pulls everything near it into the black hole. Even light can't escape!

Depending on the shape of the universe, black holes may allow us to travel great distances. They may even take us to entirely new universes. The truth is no one knows what lies on the other side of a black hole.

SUPERMASSIVE NEIGHBORS

In 2011, researchers found two supermassive black holes about 300 million light-years from Earth. The larger of the two may be the biggest black hole ever discovered. It is estimated to be 21 billion times more massive than our sun.

BLACK HOLE BREAKDOWN

Once something crosses the **event horizon**, it can't escape the pull of gravity.

A **singularity** lies at the center of every black hole. This is where all the mass that has been pulled inside collects.

Scientists believe that black hole singularities have infinite gravity. How is this possible? This is one of the mysteries they want to understand.

Just as their name suggests, black holes are actually black. Nothing—not even light—can escape from a black hole.

WORMHOLES

Scientists use math to tell them about areas of the universe that haven't been explored yet. The math seems to say there may be ways to travel great distances quickly. One way could be through a **wormhole**. A wormhole is a kind of tunnel in space. It's a shortcut that closes the distance between two different places and time periods. Scientists are studying whether there may be a way to build a wormhole. Some believe it may be possible to use wormholes to travel through space. But others believe they are like black holes. Once inside, there's no going back!

ALL AROUND US

Some scientists believe there are wormholes constantly forming all around us. They are just so tiny they can never be seen.

Some scientists think black holes may be a type of wormhole.

THE FUTURE IS OURS

Exciting discoveries await us in the 22nd century. Will a space elevator transport people to the moon? Who will be the first person to live on Mars? We can only guess what the future may hold for space travel. But the time to research and plan new technologies is now. What would you like to explore in space? What technology would you like to see? Some futurists think there may be people alive today who will live to be 200 years old. It just might be possible that you could be alive to see what happens in the future of space!

THE NEXT FRONTIER

We don't yet know what will happen in the 22nd century. But futurists have many ideas. What do you think we will accomplish next? What do you think we might find as we continue our exploration of space? Are there events you would like to add to those below?

2110?

Terraforming Mars begins.

2120?

The International Space Elevator begins taking passengers outside our atmosphere.

2100?

Sail crafts are commonly used to travel through the solar system.

???

Humans encounter intelligent alien life!

2190?

Teleportation of humans from place to place is common.

2170?

Power plants using antimatter technology are developed.

2160?

The first people to reach their 200th birthdays celebrate with 8 generations of their families!

2150?

People are able to travel to nearby star systems for the first time.

2140?

Large stationary objects can be teleported.

2130?

The terraforming of Mars is completed. Colonists begin to arrive.

GLOSSARY

aliens—beings that come from or live on another world

antimatter—the opposite of matter; matter with a negative charge

artificial gravity—a man-made force that mimics gravity

artificial intelligence (AI)—the power of a computer to imitate human behaviors and make decisions

atmosphere—the gases surrounding a planet

black holes—objects with mass so great that they have collapsed in on themselves, pulling in everything within range of their gravity, including light

breakthroughs—sudden advances in knowledge or technique

data—information

element—one of the basic pieces that make up objects in the universe

event horizon—the place in a black hole beyond which an object cannot escape the gravity of the black hole

exoplanets—planets that orbit a star other than our sun

femtotechnology—the ability to create specific atoms from subatomic particles

futurists—people who study and imagine what the future may be like

galaxy—a huge system of stars connected by gravity

genes—the unit through which traits are transferred from parent to offspring

habitable—fit to live in

intelligent life—creatures that have a set of characteristics that indicate they are alive and appear aware of their surroundings

light sail craft—spacecraft pushed by photons

morphing—changing shape

nanotechnology—the ability to build things with individual atoms and molecules

obsolete—no longer in use because something new has replaced it

overpopulation—the condition of having too many organisms living in a defined area

parallel universes—alternate realities; universes that may exist outside our own

photons—particles of energy, most often light

renewable—capable of being replaced by natural cycles

singularity—the extremely dense ball of matter at the center of a black hole

teleportation—moving things instantly from place to place

terraforming—transforming a planet to be habitable for life where it couldn't exist before

universe—everything observed or assumed to exist

wormhole—an object that may exist and act as a tunnel connecting points that are widely separated in space and time

INDEX

BIBLIOGRAPHY

Bridgman, Roger Francis. *DK Eyewitness Books: Robot.* **DK Children's Publishing, 2004.**

Explore the world of robots from inside classrooms and hospitals to science labs and outer space. This book includes a chapter on what scientists predict robots will be able to do in the future.

Close, Frank. *Antimatter.* **Oxford University Press, 2010.**

Delve into a bizarre mirror world where everything has the opposite properties to the matter in our familiar world. Antimatter is not just the stuff of science fiction, and this book tells why it may help us solve mysteries about the origins of the universe.

Greathouse, Lisa. *Astronomers Through Time.* **Teacher Created Materials, 2008.**

Learn how people first began discovering the universe. From Nicholas Copernicus to NASA's great thinkers today, scientists change the way we see the universe and our place in it.

Skurzynski, Gloria. *This Is Rocket Science: True Stories of the Risk-Taking Scientists Who Figure Out Ways to Explore Beyond Earth.* **National Geographic Society, 2010.**

Prepare to launch your imagination into outer space! This book covers the history and future of space travel. You'll learn about amazing new technologies including space elevators, solar sails, and ion propulsion.

Spangenburg, Ray and Kit Moser. *Onboard the Space Shuttle.* **Franklin Watts, 2002.**

Learn what it's like to live in space! This book focuses on the daily life of astronauts and includes a chapter on space stations so you can prepare for your future living in space.

MORE TO EXPLORE

Antimatter Orbiting Earth

http://news.nationalgeographic.com/news/2011/08/110810-antimatter
-belt-earth-trapped-pamela-space-science/

Read an article about an antimatter belt recently discovered orbiting Earth.

Black Holes

http://www.kidsastronomy.com/black_hole.htm

Explore black holes on KidsAstronomy.com. You can watch a video of an animated black hole to learn about singularities and event horizons.

Carbon Nanotubes

http://www.news.discovery.com/carbon-nanotubes/

Here, you can watch a video about nanotechnology's rewards and drawbacks. Also, read about how carbon nanotubes are changing the world.

Dark Energy, Dark Matter

http://www.science.nasa.gov/astrophysics/focus-areas/what-is-dark-energy/

Learn about dark energy and dark matter on the NASA Science website. Read about recent discoveries in these mysterious fields.

Satellite Flybys

http://www.spaceweather.com/flybys/

Enter your zip code to find out what satellites will be flying over your area. You might be able to see the International Space Station (ISS) since it's brighter than Venus and takes five minutes to cross the sky.

ABOUT THE AUTHOR

Stephanie Paris grew up in California. She received a degree in psychology from UC Santa Cruz and a teaching credential from CSU San Jose. She has been an elementary classroom teacher, an elementary school computer and technology teacher, a home-schooling mother, an educational activist, an educational author, a web designer, a blogger, and a Girl Scout leader. Ms. Paris loves to explore! She would love a chance to explore space. In the meantime, she currently lives in Germany with her husband and two children.